Dream Journal

Date:_____ Time:_____

Thoughts Before Sleep

_____
_____
_____
_____

Emotions Before Sleep

_____
_____

Dream

_____
_____
_____
_____
_____
_____
_____
_____

Interpretation

_____
_____
_____

Feeling Upon Awakening

_____
_____
_____

Comments

_____
_____
_____

Dream Journal

Date:_____   Time:_____

Thoughts Before Sleep
_____
_____
_____
_____

Emotions Before Sleep
_____

Dream
_____
_____
_____
_____
_____
_____
_____

Interpretation
_____
_____
_____

Feeling Upon Awakening
_____
_____
_____

Comments
_____
_____

Dream Journal

Date:_____   Time:_____

Thoughts Before Sleep

_____
_____
_____
_____

Emotions Before Sleep

_____

Dream

_____
_____
_____
_____
_____
_____
_____

Interpretation

_____
_____

Feeling Upon Awakening

_____
_____
_____

Comments

_____
_____

Dream Journal

Date:_____   Time:_____

Thoughts Before Sleep
_____
_____
_____
_____

Emotions Before Sleep
_____

Dream
_____
_____
_____
_____
_____
_____

Interpretation
_____
_____

Feeling Upon Awakening
_____
_____
_____

Comments
_____
_____
_____

Dream Journal

Date:_____   Time:_____

Thoughts Before Sleep
_____
_____
_____
_____

Emotions Before Sleep
_____
_____

Dream
_____
_____
_____
_____
_____
_____
_____

Interpretation
_____
_____
_____

Feeling Upon Awakening
_____
_____
_____

Comments
_____
_____
_____

Dream Journal

Date:_____   Time:_____

Thoughts Before Sleep

_____
_____
_____
_____

Emotions Before Sleep

_____

Dream

_____
_____
_____
_____
_____
_____
_____

Interpretation

_____
_____

Feeling Upon Awakening

_____
_____
_____

Comments

_____
_____

Dream Journal

Date:_____   Time:_____

Thoughts Before Sleep

_____
_____
_____
_____

Emotions Before Sleep

_____

Dream

_____
_____
_____
_____
_____
_____
_____

Interpretation

_____
_____

Feeling Upon Awakening

_____
_____
_____

Comments

_____
_____

Dream Journal

Date:_____   Time:_____

Thoughts Before Sleep

_____
_____
_____
_____

Emotions Before Sleep

_____

Dream

_____
_____
_____
_____
_____
_____
_____

Interpretation

_____
_____

Feeling Upon Awakening

_____
_____
_____

Comments

_____
_____

Dream Journal

Date:_____   Time:_____

Thoughts Before Sleep
_____
_____
_____
_____

Emotions Before Sleep
_____
_____

Dream
_____
_____
_____
_____
_____
_____
_____

Interpretation
_____
_____
_____

Feeling Upon Awakening
_____
_____
_____

Comments
_____
_____

Dream Journal

Date:_____   Time:_____

Thoughts Before Sleep

_____
_____
_____
_____

Emotions Before Sleep

_____
_____

Dream

_____
_____
_____
_____
_____
_____
_____
_____

Interpretation

_____
_____
_____

Feeling Upon Awakening

_____
_____
_____

Comments

_____
_____
_____

Dream Journal

Date:_____   Time:_____

Thoughts Before Sleep
_____
_____
_____
_____

Emotions Before Sleep
_____
_____

Dream
_____
_____
_____
_____
_____
_____
_____

Interpretation
_____
_____

Feeling Upon Awakening
_____
_____
_____

Comments
_____
_____

Dream Journal

Date:_____ Time:_____

Thoughts Before Sleep

_____
_____
_____
_____

Emotions Before Sleep

_____

Dream

_____
_____
_____
_____
_____
_____
_____
_____

Interpretation

_____
_____
_____

Feeling Upon Awakening

_____
_____
_____

Comments

_____
_____

Dream Journal

Date:_____   Time:_____

Thoughts Before Sleep
_____
_____
_____
_____

Emotions Before Sleep
_____

Dream
_____
_____
_____
_____
_____
_____
_____

Interpretation
_____
_____

Feeling Upon Awakening
_____
_____
_____

Comments
_____
_____
_____

Dream Journal

Date:_____ Time:_____

Thoughts Before Sleep

_____
_____
_____
_____

Emotions Before Sleep

_____
_____

Dream

_____
_____
_____
_____
_____
_____
_____
_____

Interpretation

_____
_____
_____

Feeling Upon Awakening

_____
_____
_____

Comments

_____
_____

Dream Journal

Date:_____   Time:_____

Thoughts Before Sleep

_____
_____
_____
_____

Emotions Before Sleep

_____
_____

Dream

_____
_____
_____
_____
_____
_____
_____

Interpretation

_____
_____

Feeling Upon Awakening

_____
_____
_____

Comments

_____
_____

Dream Journal

Date:_____   Time:_____

Thoughts Before Sleep

_____
_____
_____
_____

Emotions Before Sleep

_____

Dream

_____
_____
_____
_____
_____
_____
_____

Interpretation

_____
_____

Feeling Upon Awakening

_____
_____
_____

Comments

_____
_____
_____

Dream Journal

Date:_____   Time:_____

Thoughts Before Sleep

_____
_____
_____
_____

Emotions Before Sleep

_____

Dream

_____
_____
_____
_____
_____
_____
_____

Interpretation

_____
_____

Feeling Upon Awakening

_____
_____
_____

Comments

_____
_____

Dream Journal

Date:_____ Time:_____

Thoughts Before Sleep

_____
_____
_____
_____

Emotions Before Sleep

_____

Dream

_____
_____
_____
_____
_____
_____
_____

Interpretation

_____
_____

Feeling Upon Awakening

_____
_____
_____

Comments

_____
_____

Dream Journal

Date:_____ Time:_____

Thoughts Before Sleep

_____
_____
_____
_____

Emotions Before Sleep

_____

Dream

_____
_____
_____
_____
_____
_____

Interpretation

_____
_____

Feeling Upon Awakening

_____
_____

Comments

_____
_____

Dream Journal

Date:_____   Time:_____

Thoughts Before Sleep

_____
_____
_____
_____

Emotions Before Sleep

_____

Dream

_____
_____
_____
_____
_____
_____
_____

Interpretation

_____
_____

Feeling Upon Awakening

_____
_____
_____

Comments

_____
_____

Dream Journal

Date:_____   Time:_____

Thoughts Before Sleep

_____
_____
_____
_____

Emotions Before Sleep

_____

Dream

_____
_____
_____
_____
_____
_____
_____

Interpretation

_____
_____

Feeling Upon Awakening

_____
_____
_____

Comments

_____
_____

Dream Journal

Date:_____   Time:_____

Thoughts Before Sleep

_____
_____
_____
_____

Emotions Before Sleep

_____

Dream

_____
_____
_____
_____
_____
_____
_____

Interpretation

_____
_____

Feeling Upon Awakening

_____
_____
_____

Comments

_____
_____

Dream Journal

Date:_____ Time:_____

Thoughts Before Sleep

_____
_____
_____
_____

Emotions Before Sleep

_____

Dream

_____
_____
_____
_____
_____
_____
_____

Interpretation

_____
_____

Feeling Upon Awakening

_____
_____

Comments

_____
_____

Dream Journal

Date:_____   Time:_____

Thoughts Before Sleep

_____
_____
_____
_____

Emotions Before Sleep

_____

Dream

_____
_____
_____
_____
_____
_____
_____

Interpretation

_____
_____

Feeling Upon Awakening

_____
_____
_____

Comments

_____
_____

Dream Journal

Date:_____   Time:_____

Thoughts Before Sleep
_____
_____
_____
_____

Emotions Before Sleep
_____

Dream
_____
_____
_____
_____
_____
_____
_____
_____

Interpretation
_____
_____

Feeling Upon Awakening
_____
_____
_____

Comments
_____
_____

Dream Journal

Date:_____   Time:_____

Thoughts Before Sleep

_____
_____
_____
_____

Emotions Before Sleep

_____

Dream

_____
_____
_____
_____
_____
_____
_____

Interpretation

_____
_____

Feeling Upon Awakening

_____
_____
_____

Comments

_____
_____

Dream Journal

Date:_____ Time:_____

Thoughts Before Sleep

_____
_____
_____
_____

Emotions Before Sleep

_____

Dream

_____
_____
_____
_____
_____
_____
_____

Interpretation

_____
_____

Feeling Upon Awakening

_____
_____
_____

Comments

_____
_____

Dream Journal

Date:_____   Time:_____

Thoughts Before Sleep

_____
_____
_____
_____

Emotions Before Sleep

_____
_____

Dream

_____
_____
_____
_____
_____
_____
_____
_____

Interpretation

_____
_____
_____

Feeling Upon Awakening

_____
_____
_____

Comments

_____
_____

Dream Journal

Date:_____   Time:_____

Thoughts Before Sleep

_____
_____
_____
_____

Emotions Before Sleep

_____
_____

Dream

_____
_____
_____
_____
_____
_____
_____
_____

Interpretation

_____
_____
_____

Feeling Upon Awakening

_____
_____
_____

Comments

_____
_____

Dream Journal

Date:_____ Time:_____

Thoughts Before Sleep

_____
_____
_____
_____

Emotions Before Sleep

_____

Dream

_____
_____
_____
_____
_____
_____
_____

Interpretation

_____
_____

Feeling Upon Awakening

_____
_____
_____

Comments

_____
_____

Dream Journal

Date:_____ Time:_____

Thoughts Before Sleep

_____
_____
_____

Emotions Before Sleep

_____

Dream

_____
_____
_____
_____
_____
_____
_____

Interpretation

_____
_____

Feeling Upon Awakening

_____
_____

Comments

_____
_____

Dream Journal

Date:_____ Time:_____

Thoughts Before Sleep
_____
_____
_____
_____

Emotions Before Sleep
_____

Dream
_____
_____
_____
_____
_____
_____
_____

Interpretation
_____
_____

Feeling Upon Awakening
_____
_____
_____

Comments
_____
_____

Dream Journal

Date:_____ Time:_____

Thoughts Before Sleep

_____
_____
_____
_____

Emotions Before Sleep

_____

Dream

_____
_____
_____
_____
_____
_____
_____
_____

Interpretation

_____
_____

Feeling Upon Awakening

_____
_____
_____

Comments

_____
_____

Dream Journal

Date:_____   Time:_____

Thoughts Before Sleep

_____
_____
_____
_____

Emotions Before Sleep

_____

Dream

_____
_____
_____
_____
_____
_____
_____

Interpretation

_____
_____

Feeling Upon Awakening

_____
_____
_____

Comments

_____
_____

Dream Journal

Date:_____   Time:_____

Thoughts Before Sleep

_____
_____
_____
_____

Emotions Before Sleep

_____

Dream

_____
_____
_____
_____
_____
_____
_____

Interpretation

_____
_____

Feeling Upon Awakening

_____
_____

Comments

_____
_____

Dream Journal

Date:_____   Time:_____

Thoughts Before Sleep
_____
_____
_____
_____

Emotions Before Sleep
_____

Dream
_____
_____
_____
_____
_____
_____
_____

Interpretation
_____
_____

Feeling Upon Awakening
_____
_____
_____

Comments
_____
_____

Dream Journal

Date:_____ Time:_____

Thoughts Before Sleep

_____
_____
_____
_____

Emotions Before Sleep

_____

Dream

_____
_____
_____
_____
_____
_____
_____

Interpretation

_____
_____

Feeling Upon Awakening

_____
_____
_____

Comments

_____
_____

Dream Journal

Date:_____   Time:_____

Thoughts Before Sleep

_____
_____
_____
_____

Emotions Before Sleep

_____

Dream

_____
_____
_____
_____
_____
_____
_____

Interpretation

_____
_____

Feeling Upon Awakening

_____
_____
_____

Comments

_____
_____

Dream Journal

Date:_____   Time:_____

Thoughts Before Sleep

_____
_____
_____
_____

Emotions Before Sleep

_____

Dream

_____
_____
_____
_____
_____
_____
_____

Interpretation

_____
_____

Feeling Upon Awakening

_____
_____
_____

Comments

_____
_____

Dream Journal

Date:_____   Time:_____

Thoughts Before Sleep

_____
_____
_____
_____

Emotions Before Sleep

_____

Dream

_____
_____
_____
_____
_____
_____
_____

Interpretation

_____
_____

Feeling Upon Awakening

_____
_____
_____

Comments

_____
_____

Dream Journal

Date:_____   Time:_____

Thoughts Before Sleep

_____
_____
_____
_____

Emotions Before Sleep

_____

Dream

_____
_____
_____
_____
_____
_____
_____

Interpretation

_____
_____

Feeling Upon Awakening

_____
_____

Comments

_____
_____

Dream Journal

Date:_____   Time:_____

Thoughts Before Sleep

_____
_____
_____
_____

Emotions Before Sleep

_____
_____

Dream

_____
_____
_____
_____
_____
_____
_____
_____

Interpretation

_____
_____
_____

Feeling Upon Awakening

_____
_____
_____

Comments

_____
_____
_____

Dream Journal

Date:_____   Time:_____

Thoughts Before Sleep

_____
_____
_____
_____

Emotions Before Sleep

_____

Dream

_____
_____
_____
_____
_____
_____
_____

Interpretation

_____
_____

Feeling Upon Awakening

_____
_____
_____

Comments

_____
_____

Dream Journal

Date:_____ Time:_____

Thoughts Before Sleep

_____
_____
_____
_____

Emotions Before Sleep

_____

Dream

_____
_____
_____
_____
_____
_____
_____

Interpretation

_____
_____

Feeling Upon Awakening

_____
_____
_____

Comments

_____
_____

Dream Journal

Date:_____   Time:_____

Thoughts Before Sleep

_____
_____
_____
_____

Emotions Before Sleep

_____

Dream

_____
_____
_____
_____
_____
_____
_____

Interpretation

_____
_____

Feeling Upon Awakening

_____
_____

Comments

_____
_____

Dream Journal

Date:_____   Time:_____

Thoughts Before Sleep
_____
_____
_____
_____

Emotions Before Sleep
_____

Dream
_____
_____
_____
_____
_____
_____
_____

Interpretation
_____
_____

Feeling Upon Awakening
_____
_____
_____

Comments
_____
_____

Dream Journal

Date:_____ Time:_____

Thoughts Before Sleep

_____
_____
_____
_____

Emotions Before Sleep

_____

Dream

_____
_____
_____
_____
_____
_____
_____

Interpretation

_____
_____

Feeling Upon Awakening

_____
_____
_____

Comments

_____
_____

Dream Journal

Date:_____ Time:_____

Thoughts Before Sleep

_____
_____
_____
_____

Emotions Before Sleep

_____

Dream

_____
_____
_____
_____
_____
_____
_____

Interpretation

_____
_____
_____

Feeling Upon Awakening

_____
_____
_____

Comments

_____
_____

Dream Journal

Date:_____   Time:_____

Thoughts Before Sleep

_____
_____
_____
_____

Emotions Before Sleep

_____

Dream

_____
_____
_____
_____
_____
_____
_____

Interpretation

_____
_____

Feeling Upon Awakening

_____
_____

Comments

_____
_____

Dream Journal

Date:_____   Time:_____

Thoughts Before Sleep

_____
_____
_____
_____

Emotions Before Sleep

_____

Dream

_____
_____
_____
_____
_____
_____
_____

Interpretation

_____
_____

Feeling Upon Awakening

_____
_____
_____

Comments

_____
_____

Dream Journal

Date:_____ Time:_____

Thoughts Before Sleep

_____
_____
_____
_____

Emotions Before Sleep

_____

Dream

_____
_____
_____
_____
_____
_____
_____

Interpretation

_____
_____

Feeling Upon Awakening

_____
_____
_____

Comments

_____
_____

Dream Journal

Date:_____   Time:_____

Thoughts Before Sleep

_____
_____
_____
_____

Emotions Before Sleep

_____

Dream

_____
_____
_____
_____
_____
_____
_____

Interpretation

_____
_____

Feeling Upon Awakening

_____
_____
_____

Comments

_____
_____

Dream Journal

Date:_____   Time:_____

Thoughts Before Sleep

_____
_____
_____
_____

Emotions Before Sleep

_____

Dream

_____
_____
_____
_____
_____
_____
_____

Interpretation

_____
_____

Feeling Upon Awakening

_____
_____
_____

Comments

_____
_____

Dream Journal

Date:_____   Time:_____

Thoughts Before Sleep

_____
_____
_____

Emotions Before Sleep

_____

Dream

_____
_____
_____
_____
_____
_____

Interpretation

_____
_____

Feeling Upon Awakening

_____
_____
_____

Comments

_____
_____
_____

Dream Journal

Date:_____   Time:_____

Thoughts Before Sleep

_____
_____
_____
_____

Emotions Before Sleep

_____

Dream

_____
_____
_____
_____
_____
_____
_____

Interpretation

_____
_____

Feeling Upon Awakening

_____
_____
_____

Comments

_____
_____

Dream Journal

Date:_____ Time:_____

Thoughts Before Sleep

_____
_____
_____
_____

Emotions Before Sleep

_____

Dream

_____
_____
_____
_____
_____
_____
_____

Interpretation

_____
_____
_____

Feeling Upon Awakening

_____
_____
_____

Comments

_____
_____

Dream Journal

Date:_____   Time:_____

Thoughts Before Sleep

_____
_____
_____
_____

Emotions Before Sleep

_____
_____

Dream

_____
_____
_____
_____
_____
_____
_____
_____

Interpretation

_____
_____
_____

Feeling Upon Awakening

_____
_____
_____

Comments

_____
_____

Dream Journal

Date:_____ Time:_____

Thoughts Before Sleep

_____
_____
_____
_____
_____

Emotions Before Sleep

_____

Dream

_____
_____
_____
_____
_____
_____
_____
_____

Interpretation

_____
_____

Feeling Upon Awakening

_____
_____
_____

Comments

_____
_____

Dream Journal

Date:_____   Time:_____

Thoughts Before Sleep

_____
_____
_____
_____

Emotions Before Sleep

_____

Dream

_____
_____
_____
_____
_____
_____
_____

Interpretation

_____
_____
_____

Feeling Upon Awakening

_____
_____
_____

Comments

_____
_____
_____

Dream Journal

Date:_____   Time:_____

Thoughts Before Sleep

_____
_____
_____
_____

Emotions Before Sleep

_____

Dream

_____
_____
_____
_____
_____
_____
_____

Interpretation

_____
_____

Feeling Upon Awakening

_____
_____
_____

Comments

_____
_____

Dream Journal

Date:_____ Time:_____

Thoughts Before Sleep

_____
_____
_____
_____

Emotions Before Sleep

_____

Dream

_____
_____
_____
_____
_____
_____
_____

Interpretation

_____
_____
_____

Feeling Upon Awakening

_____
_____
_____

Comments

_____
_____

Dream Journal

Date:_____ Time:_____

Thoughts Before Sleep

_____
_____
_____
_____

Emotions Before Sleep

_____

Dream

_____
_____
_____
_____
_____
_____
_____

Interpretation

_____
_____
_____

Feeling Upon Awakening

_____
_____
_____

Comments

_____
_____
_____

Dream Journal

Date:_____   Time:_____

Thoughts Before Sleep

_____
_____
_____
_____

Emotions Before Sleep

_____

Dream

_____
_____
_____
_____
_____
_____
_____

Interpretation

_____
_____

Feeling Upon Awakening

_____
_____
_____

Comments

_____
_____

Dream Journal

Date:_____   Time:_____

Thoughts Before Sleep

_____
_____
_____
_____

Emotions Before Sleep

_____

Dream

_____
_____
_____
_____
_____
_____
_____

Interpretation

_____
_____

Feeling Upon Awakening

_____
_____
_____

Comments

_____
_____

Dream Journal

Date:_____ Time:_____

Thoughts Before Sleep

_____
_____
_____
_____

Emotions Before Sleep

_____

Dream

_____
_____
_____
_____
_____
_____
_____

Interpretation

_____
_____

Feeling Upon Awakening

_____
_____
_____

Comments

_____
_____
_____

Dream Journal

Date:_____   Time:_____

Thoughts Before Sleep

_____
_____
_____
_____

Emotions Before Sleep

_____

Dream

_____
_____
_____
_____
_____
_____
_____
_____

Interpretation

_____
_____

Feeling Upon Awakening

_____
_____
_____

Comments

_____
_____

Dream Journal

Date:_____   Time:_____

Thoughts Before Sleep

_____
_____
_____
_____

Emotions Before Sleep

_____
_____

Dream

_____
_____
_____
_____
_____
_____
_____
_____

Interpretation

_____
_____
_____

Feeling Upon Awakening

_____
_____
_____

Comments

_____
_____
_____

Dream Journal

Date:_____ Time:_____

Thoughts Before Sleep

Emotions Before Sleep

Dream

Interpretation

Feeling Upon Awakening

Comments

Dream Journal

Date:_____   Time:_____

Thoughts Before Sleep

_____
_____
_____
_____

Emotions Before Sleep

_____

Dream

_____
_____
_____
_____
_____
_____
_____
_____

Interpretation

_____
_____

Feeling Upon Awakening

_____
_____

Comments

_____
_____

Dream Journal

Date:_____ Time:_____

Thoughts Before Sleep

_____
_____
_____

Emotions Before Sleep

_____

Dream

_____
_____
_____
_____
_____
_____

Interpretation

_____
_____

Feeling Upon Awakening

_____
_____

Comments

_____
_____

Dream Journal

Date:_____   Time:_____

Thoughts Before Sleep

_____
_____
_____
_____

Emotions Before Sleep

_____

Dream

_____
_____
_____
_____
_____
_____
_____

Interpretation

_____
_____
_____

Feeling Upon Awakening

_____
_____
_____

Comments

_____
_____

Dream Journal

Date:_____   Time:_____

Thoughts Before Sleep

_____
_____
_____
_____

Emotions Before Sleep

_____

Dream

_____
_____
_____
_____
_____
_____
_____

Interpretation

_____
_____

Feeling Upon Awakening

_____
_____
_____

Comments

_____
_____

Dream Journal

Date:_____   Time:_____

Thoughts Before Sleep

_____
_____
_____
_____

Emotions Before Sleep

_____

Dream

_____
_____
_____
_____
_____
_____
_____
_____

Interpretation

_____
_____

Feeling Upon Awakening

_____
_____
_____

Comments

_____
_____

Dream Journal

Date:_____   Time:_____

Thoughts Before Sleep

_____
_____
_____
_____

Emotions Before Sleep

_____

Dream

_____
_____
_____
_____
_____
_____
_____

Interpretation

_____
_____

Feeling Upon Awakening

_____
_____
_____

Comments

_____
_____

Dream Journal

Date:_____   Time:_____

Thoughts Before Sleep

_____
_____
_____
_____

Emotions Before Sleep

_____

Dream

_____
_____
_____
_____
_____
_____
_____

Interpretation

_____
_____
_____

Feeling Upon Awakening

_____
_____
_____

Comments

_____
_____

Dream Journal

Date:_____   Time:_____

Thoughts Before Sleep

_____
_____
_____
_____

Emotions Before Sleep

_____

Dream

_____
_____
_____
_____
_____
_____
_____

Interpretation

_____
_____

Feeling Upon Awakening

_____
_____
_____

Comments

_____
_____

Dream Journal

Date:_____   Time:_____

Thoughts Before Sleep

_____
_____
_____
_____
_____

Emotions Before Sleep

_____
_____

Dream

_____
_____
_____
_____
_____
_____
_____
_____

Interpretation

_____
_____

Feeling Upon Awakening

_____
_____
_____

Comments

_____
_____

Dream Journal

Date:_____   Time:_____

Thoughts Before Sleep

_____
_____
_____
_____

Emotions Before Sleep

_____

Dream

_____
_____
_____
_____
_____
_____
_____

Interpretation

_____
_____

Feeling Upon Awakening

_____
_____
_____

Comments

_____
_____

Dream Journal

Date:_____   Time:_____

Thoughts Before Sleep

_____
_____
_____
_____
_____

Emotions Before Sleep

_____

Dream

_____
_____
_____
_____
_____
_____
_____
_____

Interpretation

_____
_____
_____

Feeling Upon Awakening

_____
_____
_____

Comments

_____
_____

Dream Journal

Date:_____   Time:_____

Thoughts Before Sleep

_____
_____
_____
_____
_____

Emotions Before Sleep

_____
_____

Dream

_____
_____
_____
_____
_____
_____
_____
_____

Interpretation

_____
_____
_____

Feeling Upon Awakening

_____
_____
_____

Comments

_____
_____

Dream Journal

Date:_____   Time:_____

Thoughts Before Sleep
_____
_____
_____
_____

Emotions Before Sleep
_____

Dream
_____
_____
_____
_____
_____
_____
_____

Interpretation
_____
_____

Feeling Upon Awakening
_____
_____
_____

Comments
_____
_____

Dream Journal

Date:_____ Time:_____

Thoughts Before Sleep

Emotions Before Sleep

Dream

Interpretation

Feeling Upon Awakening

Comments

Dream Journal

Date:_____   Time:_____

Thoughts Before Sleep

_____
_____
_____
_____

Emotions Before Sleep

_____

Dream

_____
_____
_____
_____
_____
_____
_____

Interpretation

_____
_____
_____

Feeling Upon Awakening

_____
_____
_____

Comments

_____
_____

Dream Journal

Date:_____   Time:_____

Thoughts Before Sleep

_____
_____
_____
_____

Emotions Before Sleep

_____
_____

Dream

_____
_____
_____
_____
_____
_____
_____
_____

Interpretation

_____
_____
_____

Feeling Upon Awakening

_____
_____
_____

Comments

_____
_____
_____

Dream Journal

Date:_____   Time:_____

Thoughts Before Sleep

_____
_____
_____
_____

Emotions Before Sleep

_____

Dream

_____
_____
_____
_____
_____
_____
_____

Interpretation

_____
_____

Feeling Upon Awakening

_____
_____
_____

Comments

_____
_____

Dream Journal

Date:_____ Time:_____

Thoughts Before Sleep

_____
_____
_____
_____

Emotions Before Sleep

_____

Dream

_____
_____
_____
_____
_____
_____
_____

Interpretation

_____
_____

Feeling Upon Awakening

_____
_____
_____

Comments

_____
_____
_____

Dream Journal

Date:_____ Time:_____

Thoughts Before Sleep

_____
_____
_____
_____

Emotions Before Sleep

_____
_____

Dream

_____
_____
_____
_____
_____
_____
_____

Interpretation

_____
_____
_____

Feeling Upon Awakening

_____
_____
_____

Comments

_____
_____

Dream Journal

Date:_____   Time:_____

Thoughts Before Sleep
_____
_____
_____
_____

Emotions Before Sleep
_____

Dream
_____
_____
_____
_____
_____
_____
_____

Interpretation
_____
_____

Feeling Upon Awakening
_____
_____
_____

Comments
_____
_____

Dream Journal

Date:_____ Time:_____

Thoughts Before Sleep

_____
_____
_____
_____

Emotions Before Sleep

_____

Dream

_____
_____
_____
_____
_____
_____
_____

Interpretation

_____
_____

Feeling Upon Awakening

_____
_____
_____

Comments

_____
_____

Dream Journal

Date:_____   Time:_____

Thoughts Before Sleep

_____
_____
_____
_____

Emotions Before Sleep

_____

Dream

_____
_____
_____
_____
_____
_____
_____

Interpretation

_____
_____

Feeling Upon Awakening

_____
_____
_____

Comments

_____
_____

Dream Journal

Date:_____   Time:_____

Thoughts Before Sleep
_____
_____
_____
_____

Emotions Before Sleep
_____
_____

Dream
_____
_____
_____
_____
_____
_____
_____

Interpretation
_____
_____
_____

Feeling Upon Awakening
_____
_____
_____

Comments
_____
_____

Dream Journal

Date:_____   Time:_____

Thoughts Before Sleep

_____
_____
_____
_____

Emotions Before Sleep

_____

Dream

_____
_____
_____
_____
_____
_____
_____

Interpretation

_____
_____

Feeling Upon Awakening

_____
_____
_____

Comments

_____
_____

Dream Journal

Date:_____   Time:_____

Thoughts Before Sleep

_____
_____
_____
_____

Emotions Before Sleep

_____

Dream

_____
_____
_____
_____
_____
_____
_____

Interpretation

_____
_____

Feeling Upon Awakening

_____
_____
_____

Comments

_____
_____

Dream Journal

Date:_____   Time:_____

Thoughts Before Sleep

_____
_____
_____
_____

Emotions Before Sleep

_____
_____

Dream

_____
_____
_____
_____
_____
_____
_____

Interpretation

_____
_____

Feeling Upon Awakening

_____
_____
_____

Comments

_____
_____

Dream Journal

Date:_____ Time:_____

Thoughts Before Sleep

_____
_____
_____
_____
_____

Emotions Before Sleep

_____

Dream

_____
_____
_____
_____
_____
_____
_____

Interpretation

_____
_____

Feeling Upon Awakening

_____
_____
_____

Comments

_____
_____

Dream Journal

Date:_____   Time:_____

Thoughts Before Sleep

_____
_____
_____
_____

Emotions Before Sleep

_____

Dream

_____
_____
_____
_____
_____
_____
_____

Interpretation

_____
_____

Feeling Upon Awakening

_____
_____
_____

Comments

_____
_____

Dream Journal

Date:_____   Time:_____

Thoughts Before Sleep

_____
_____
_____
_____

Emotions Before Sleep

_____

Dream

_____
_____
_____
_____
_____
_____
_____

Interpretation

_____
_____

Feeling Upon Awakening

_____
_____
_____

Comments

_____
_____

Dream Journal

Date:_____ Time:_____

Thoughts Before Sleep

_____
_____
_____
_____

Emotions Before Sleep

_____

Dream

_____
_____
_____
_____
_____
_____
_____

Interpretation

_____
_____

Feeling Upon Awakening

_____
_____
_____

Comments

_____
_____

Dream Journal

Date:_____   Time:_____

Thoughts Before Sleep

_____
_____
_____
_____

Emotions Before Sleep

_____

Dream

_____
_____
_____
_____
_____
_____
_____

Interpretation

_____
_____

Feeling Upon Awakening

_____
_____
_____

Comments

_____
_____
_____

Dream Journal

Date:_____   Time:_____

Thoughts Before Sleep

_____
_____
_____
_____

Emotions Before Sleep

_____

Dream

_____
_____
_____
_____
_____
_____
_____

Interpretation

_____
_____

Feeling Upon Awakening

_____
_____
_____

Comments

_____
_____
_____

Dream Journal

Date:_____   Time:_____

Thoughts Before Sleep

_____
_____
_____
_____

Emotions Before Sleep

_____
_____

Dream

_____
_____
_____
_____
_____
_____
_____
_____

Interpretation

_____
_____
_____

Feeling Upon Awakening

_____
_____
_____
_____

Comments

_____
_____
_____

Dream Journal

Date:_____   Time:_____

Thoughts Before Sleep

_____
_____
_____
_____

Emotions Before Sleep

_____
_____

Dream

_____
_____
_____
_____
_____
_____
_____

Interpretation

_____
_____
_____

Feeling Upon Awakening

_____
_____
_____
_____

Comments

_____
_____
_____

Dream Journal

Date:_____   Time:_____

Thoughts Before Sleep

_____
_____
_____
_____

Emotions Before Sleep

_____

Dream

_____
_____
_____
_____
_____
_____
_____

Interpretation

_____
_____
_____

Feeling Upon Awakening

_____
_____
_____

Comments

_____
_____
_____

Dream Journal

Date:_____ Time:_____

Thoughts Before Sleep

_____
_____
_____
_____

Emotions Before Sleep

_____

Dream

_____
_____
_____
_____
_____
_____
_____

Interpretation

_____
_____

Feeling Upon Awakening

_____
_____
_____

Comments

_____
_____

Dream Journal

Date:_____   Time:_____

Thoughts Before Sleep

_____
_____
_____
_____

Emotions Before Sleep

_____
_____

Dream

_____
_____
_____
_____
_____
_____
_____
_____

Interpretation

_____
_____
_____

Feeling Upon Awakening

_____
_____
_____

Comments

_____
_____

Dream Journal

Date:_____   Time:_____

Thoughts Before Sleep

_____
_____
_____
_____

Emotions Before Sleep

_____

Dream

_____
_____
_____
_____
_____
_____
_____

Interpretation

_____
_____

Feeling Upon Awakening

_____
_____
_____

Comments

_____
_____

Dream Journal

Date:_____ Time:_____

Thoughts Before Sleep

_____
_____
_____
_____

Emotions Before Sleep

_____

Dream

_____
_____
_____
_____
_____
_____
_____

Interpretation

_____
_____

Feeling Upon Awakening

_____
_____
_____

Comments

_____
_____

Dream Journal

Date:_____ Time:_____

Thoughts Before Sleep

_____
_____
_____
_____

Emotions Before Sleep

_____

Dream

_____
_____
_____
_____
_____
_____
_____

Interpretation

_____
_____

Feeling Upon Awakening

_____
_____
_____

Comments

_____
_____

Dream Journal

Date:_____ Time:_____

Thoughts Before Sleep

_____
_____
_____
_____

Emotions Before Sleep

_____

Dream

_____
_____
_____
_____
_____
_____
_____

Interpretation

_____
_____

Feeling Upon Awakening

_____
_____
_____

Comments

_____
_____

Dream Journal

Date:_____ Time:_____

Thoughts Before Sleep

_____
_____
_____
_____

Emotions Before Sleep

_____

Dream

_____
_____
_____
_____
_____
_____

Interpretation

_____
_____

Feeling Upon Awakening

_____
_____

Comments

_____
_____

Printed in Great Britain
by Amazon